Management
secrets

The experts tell all!

About the author
Michael Heath is Managing Director of Michael Heath Consulting, a Learning and Development Consultancy established in 1999. Drawing upon nearly 20 years experience of working with an impressive portfolio of international organizations, he offers a wealth of practical knowledge and insights to address the challenges that managers face. He is the author of *Leadership*, also in the **business secrets** series.

Management
secrets

Collins

A division of HarperCollins*Publishers*

77-85 Fulham Palace Road, London W6 8JB

www.BusinessSecrets.net

First published in Great Britain in 2010 by HarperCollins*Publishers*
Published in Canada by HarperCollins*Canada*. www.harpercollins.ca
Published in Australia by HarperCollins*Australia*. www.harpercollins.com.au
Published in India by HarperCollins*PublishersIndia*. www.harpercollins.co.in

1

Copyright © HarperCollins*Publishers* 2010

Michael Heath asserts the moral right to be identified as the author of this work.

A catalogue record for this book is available from the British Library.

ISBN 978-0-00-732806-2

Printed and bound at Clays Ltd, St Ives plc

Contents

Prepare to manage!

You local bookshop is stuffed full of books claiming to help you manage better. So why add one more? Because I've done the job. And I've written it so that you get quick practical advice about the every day challenges I know you face. If you think academic theories are going to help – this ain't the book.

As well as doing the job, I've spent the last 20 years or so working with other people also doing the job of management. Training them. Coaching them. Mentoring them. And believe me, that's a lot of experience to dip into. I've seen the superstar managers - and the managers who would only get a star for being so bad at it. And what separates them? Simple - great managers prepare.

So I want you to prepare to make your management life easier. I want you to experience the thrill of knowing you manage your team well. And I want you to have a reputation as the sort of manager that people imitate. That people want to be like. That's why I'm sharing these 50 **secrets** with you. You'll find these **secrets** spread over seven chapters:

■ **Manage yourself.** You've got to have a clear sense of who you are before you manage others. Personal credibility is a big factor in a manager's success.

■ **Empower your people.** People can be powerful – but only when the right management behaviours enable them to tap into that power. How you prepare for crucial interactions with others will determine your success.

■ **Make things happen.** A manager gets things done. Getting things done means applying the right tools and techniques that make sure the right things get done.

■ **Communicate in all directions.** Many don't realise just how much skill a talented manager uses when they communicate. Not just to the team, but every key person they interact with.

■ **Recruit the very best.** You want a great candidate to say 'yes' to your job offer. A systematic approach to recruitment makes this a reality.

■ **Build a great team.** Great teams don't happen by chance. A manager works carefully on the composition, skills and motivation of their employees. And they also turn team meetings into events that people look forward to.

■ **Treat the budget with respect.** Whether you've a budget or not, you will make crucial decisions that affect it. Understanding something of the process will help guide your decision making.

Time and again I'm going to talk about the need to prepare. Don't short-change yourself on this. Thinking about and preparing for the management situations you face is often the deciding factor between the great manager and the mediocre.

Great managers anticipate and prepare while others merely react and repair.

Manage yourself

I love the saying, "That which I understand, I control. That which I don't understand, controls me." This chapter is about deepening the understanding you have of yourself and how you come across to your team. These secrets address subjects that many managers do not get right. So give the questions serious thought and decide how successfully you manage yourself. Then you'll be ready to move on to managing others.

1.1

Be a role model manager

Role modelling starts when you're a child, when you start to look around for someone to copy. As you get older you start to move your target. You want to be more like your friends, your heroes, your boss…

Guess what? There are people who want to be a manager like you. To do what you do. They watch you closely and even start dealing with stuff the way that you deal with stuff. Recognize it? You probably do it yourself. You're either using approaches that your boss uses - or making sure you do the opposite!

■ **What's the great thing about role modelling?** Role modelling is imitating the success we see because we want to be successful. Well,

> **case study** At the start of my training career I delivered a workshop for my organization's customer services staff. We covered the usual things, including how you pick the phone up to customers using a proper company greeting. A few days later I was surprised to find a delegate from the workshop

"Example is not the main thing in influencing others. It is the only thing" Albert Schweitzer, German-French philosopher

if you want your people to be enthusiastic, attentive to detail, great time managers, hard working, etc., then you have to be enthusiastic, attentive to detail, a great time manager... I'm sure you've got it.

■ **The flip-side.** You can't ask your employees to do things you're not prepared to do. Need people occasionally to work late? Then you need to be seen occasionally working late. Want them to meet your deadlines? Then keep your deadlines with them. Want people to show respect for each other in the team? Then you must show respect to everyone – inside or outside the team.

By demonstrating high performance behaviour, you'll be challenging your employees to raise their game. You don't have to say, "Be more like me". They'll soon pick up the message.

Demonstrate excellence and professionalism at all times.

picking up an incoming call with a casual "Hello." I asked why he hadn't used the professional greeting we agreed on the workshop. He pointed to his boss on the other side of the room and said, "As soon as he starts answering the phone properly, I'll start answering the phone properly".

1.2

Be the real thing

It doesn't take long for people to spot a fraud. You've probably already spotted one or two at work yourself and already know how important it is to be authentic and honest with employees. But how do you build the real trust between manager and staff?

What your team wants from you is consistent behaviour. They need to see an underlying logic to your decision making. They need to feel that you are always fair – even if they don't like a decision.

This consistency always comes from a stable character. But what is character? Character is usually a combination of the qualities that make up an individual. Some qualities can be attributes such as 'determined', 'persevering' or 'enthusiastic'. Other qualities are more to do with your moral code: 'honesty', 'integrity', 'fairness'.

case study A recently promoted manager called me to ask for advice. "The trouble is I don't do small talk, Michael. I know that managers should, but it's just not what I'm good at." "Then let them know" I suggested. "Sit them down and tell them what your strengths are. Then tell them what you don't do.

Now do the following exercise:

1 **Identify your character traits.** Take a sheet of paper and write all of the qualities you believe you have. Try to identify at least 10 to 15 traits.

2 **Agree the traits.** Show these traits to someone who knows you well. A partner, friend or colleague who will give an honest opinion.

3 **Mentally 'sign up' to these character traits.** Make a pact with yourself that this is the 'real you' and the behaviour you will always try to demonstrate.

4 **Keep these traits with you.** Put the list in a discreet place where you can quickly find it.

5 **Use this list of character traits for your tough decisions.** Next time you have a tough thing to do, make sure that it reflects the character traits you signed up to.

Your employees may question your decisions but should never have cause to question your character.

They'll understand." And they did. I also think they appreciated her honesty. She started off being truthful from the start. She avoided pretending to show a quality that she didn't really have. But she showed a great quality that she did have: always wanting to be honest with her team.

1.3

Look like you mean it

Managers seldom talk about their 'image' but let's be clear: you have one. The way you dress provides visual clues to the sort of person you are. Casual dress may be cool, but smart casual is coolest of all. Think about it. You don't deliver thousand-dollar messages in one-dollar suits.

Perhaps you think I might be overestimating the impact of your appearance? Then let me point you to the election race between Richard Nixon and John F Kennedy in 1960. People still say the reason JFK won was because Nixon hadn't bothered to shave. The people in make-up couldn't hide his 5 o'clock shadow. You don't win trust looking like a gangster.

one minute wonder Look around for someone else in your organization who always manages their image well. How do they do it? What are the ways that they make sure they look the part? What can you learn from them and introduce as part of your own appearance?

"Most things are judged by their jackets"

Baltasar Gracián y Morales, 17th-century Spanish writer

■ **So what does smart dress do?** It neutralizes people's opinion of you. Instead of concentrating on your ill-fitting trousers or joke tie they concentrate on you and your message. When you dress professionally, then people assume you are a professional. You look the part.

■ **Image doesn't stop with clothes.** Looking well groomed equally sends positive messages out about you. It tells people you care about the small stuff and that detail matters. So if you travel in a car, make sure it's tidy. When you open your briefcase, don't lift the lid on a mass of papers and clutter. If your cell phone or mobile rings, don't have a ringtone that's so awful people make remarks about it.

■ **Last of all, what about your desk?** You must make sure that you look like you have everything under control. Remember, a manager's job is often about managing detail. An untidy desk sends out the wrong messages to your staff and colleagues.

All managers sell. We sell ideas, opinions and concepts. But, as any salesperson will tell you, people buy people. How you look either helps - or gets in the way of - that process.

Like it or not, people are going to judge you on your appearance.

1.4

Go on – assert yourself!

Being the boss doesn't mean being bossy. It means dealing with difficult situations fairly and skilfully. Aggression may get quick results, but you soon lose respect and loyalty. Asserting yourself is different. It's about getting your point across but keeping people with you. Being strong – but always being fair.

■ **You are going to have to deal with conflict.** It's part of what we managers do. But you can still say what you want to say and keep the respect others have for you. How? By making sure that you show respect to others.

■ **There's a big difference between aggressive and assertive managers.** Aggressive managers make their point – but in a way that ignores the rights and feelings of the person they are talking to. The

case study Two colleagues, Dev and Suki, argued and ended up not speaking to each other. Both complained separately to the manager and demanded that she deal with the situation. Unfortunately, the manager decided that they were "two adults and should sort it out between themselves".

> **"**He who conquers others is strong; He who conquers himself is mighty**"** **Lao Tzu, Taoist philosopher of ancient China**

person then feels hurt and resents the manager. Worst of all, they may even show this through sabotage and non-co-operation. An assertive manager can make the same point – but makes sure that they respect the rights of who they are speaking to.

Let me show you. I could have a disagreement and say, "You don't know what you're talking about". Notice how this not only passes judgement on the message, it passes judgement on the person as well. How much better this might be if I said, "I'd like to talk about where we disagree". This time I'm concentrating on the facts, not the person. This is why assertive people are so strong – they have a need to get at the truth, but make sure they don't make enemies when they do so.

Dealing assertively with conflict is an important skill every successful manager must master.

But over the next few months the situation just got worse. What was the result? Not only did both Dev and Suki eventually leave, but two other colleagues left as well, fed up with the bad atmosphere! Because the manager was afraid to deal properly with the situation, things got much worse.

1.5

Make time to manage

People used to worry about keeping their desk tidy.
Now it's also about keeping the computer desktop
tidy. Then there are the interruptions, the telephone,
the meetings... Follow these nine tips to get rid of the
time robbers in your life.

1 **Be clear about what you want to achieve.** Do the one minute wonder exercise opposite.

2 **Plan your work.** Write down your goals and break each goal down into sub-tasks. Give start and finish dates to each task.

3 **Book appointments with your work.** If a report is going to take two hours, then make an appointment with that report as if it were a real person.

4 **Deal with tasks as soon as you can.** If it's an unpleasant task then do it first thing.

5 **Be ruthless with time – but courteous with people.** But don't over-socialize either face to face or on the phone. Remember you're eating into other people's time as well!

one minute wonder Write down your job purpose. Then write the five activities that help you achieve this job purpose. Rate each activity 1–5 according to how happy you are with the time you spend on each (1=low, 5=high). Now get those low- rated activities into your diary!

6 **Deal with your email three times a day.** First thing in the morning, mid-morning and mid-afternoon. Turn off the pop-up that tells you when an email has just come through.

7 **Deal with interruptions.** Ask the interrupter if it's quick or if it can wait until later. If interrupted at your desk, then stand up to keep the other person focused.

8 **Deal with your in-tray once a day.** Take each item and: deal with it; delegate it; file it or dump it.

9 **Plan your telephone calls.** Save them up and do them in a block so they'll be quicker and more focused.

The worst feeling as a manager is when we think that the workload is too much for us. These nine tips make sure that you stay in control and go home each evening feeling on top of your workload.

Being a great time manager leaves you with more time for your people.

Empower your people

Now it's time to turn to the people you are managing. This chapter asks you to think about the individual interactions you have every day. Coaching and training are key managerial behaviours. Keeping your staff motivated is also crucial. Also included are secrets to dealing with tricky situations that, if handled badly, may lead to poor performance from your employees.

2.1

Manage with style

Everybody in your team is different. One might have more ability; another might have a better attitude. Some you can leave to get on with tasks; others you need to oversee more closely. Because each person is an individual, you manage each in an individual way.

The managerial approach laid out here is adapted from Ken Blanchard and Paul Hersey's *Situational Leadership* model. If you're a new manager, then it's a great starting place. You'll find their book in the 'Further Reading' section at the back.

Say to yourself: what is it my employees need from me? They need direction and they need support. Sometimes I give both, at other times only one, and sometimes neither!

What is it that helps me decide?

■ **Assess personal confidence.** I first assess how high their confidence is in a situation. If it's low, then I'll consider how best I might support them to build their self-belief.

■ **Assess personal ability.** How competent are they in this situation? Have they got the skills? Do I need to think about training or offering advice?

What if I have a person who lacks confidence and is also not yet competent? Then I use a style that gives a clear direction, yet is also supportive and encouraging. A newly promoted person often needs this. Of course, as their competence grows, so will their confidence.

Perhaps someone is confident but has done something wrong? Then they only need direction. I might coach them. Work with them to make sure they see where they might have got it wrong. You'll get people who are great performers but who lack confidence. Here I'm supportive. I remind them of what a great job they're doing.

Of course you sometimes use all four different approaches with the same person. That's the skill. Seeing the situation clearly and choosing the right managerial behaviour.

What does a high flyer need? Not much really, but I'd take the time to let them know I appreciate them. They don't need more self confidence or direction – they probably need promoting!

Your management style must respond to each individual's ability and self confidence.

2.2

Know the 'High Five' that will motivate

A motivated team looks at obstacles as things to be overcome. A demotivated team sees the same obstacles as proof of the pointlessness of their efforts. Here are my 'High Five' tips to deliver sky-high levels of motivation.

1 **Give recognition and praise for what your people achieve.** Catch people doing things right. Give the praise quickly and make sure you say why it was important.

2 **Make the work challenging.** People who are stretched maintain higher levels of motivation than people who are underused. Get your people out of their comfort zones!

3 **Make the work interesting.** We all find different work interesting. The trick is to get to know what work is interesting to each individual in your team.

"Really great people make you feel that you, too, can become great" **Mark Twain, American writer**

4 **Create development paths.** Are your people doing the same things they were doing this time last year? Then they are unlikely to be developing new skills.

5 **Encourage real ownership and responsibility.** When I own something I have more incentive to make sure I'm doing it to a high standard. Delegate whole tasks where you can. Make sure you've read our seven 'must do' delegation tips (2.6)!

If you're a good manager you'll know that there are some real 'turn-offs' that demotivate people. But demotivated people don't always tell you what it is that's demotivating them. So you have to make sure you find out. Ask things such as "What is the biggest factor that prevents you from achieving your goals?" My bet is that a big demotivator will soon emerge.

Some demotivators you can deal with and some you can't. Be creative and try and see the situation from the employee's point of view. Tackle the demotivators together. Sometimes just being listened to is enough to get them fired up again.

Mastering motivation takes time and insight, but the contribution it unleashes can be amazing.

2.3

Training is a chance to grow your own

Someone once remarked, "Everyone asks about the cost of training. But have they ever considered the cost of not training?" Nobody's good at everything. That's why a manager takes the time to train his or her people. But you must be systematic in the way you train. Even when it's only one-to-one.

Always prepare for the training session. Define the training objective in a single sentence. For example: "By the end of the session you will be able to locate a given file in a server within one minute." Notice the measurement? It's vital if you are going to encourage a sense of achievement.

Next, decide exactly how you're going to structure your session. Don't ignore this. Effective trainers know that time spent on this increases the session's success. Will you need equipment? Where would be the best place to train?

> **"What nobler employment...than that of the man who instructs the rising generation"**

Marcus Tullius Cicero, Ancient Roman philosopher

On the day itself, make sure you go through the following steps:

■ **Clarify with the trainee(s) what they are about to learn.** Tell them the objective you prepared for the session.

■ **Demonstrate the skill.** Let them see the whole skill. Then repeat it slowly. Explain what you are doing and why it's important.

■ **Do the exercise together.** This isn't always possible. But if you can go through it at the same time it's a great way to transfer a skill.

■ **Ask them to do the exercise alone.** Also ask them to talk through the process. Listen out for what they say – and what they miss out!

■ **Give helpful feedback.** Direct your feedback at the skill and not the trainee. Make sure you praise and encourage throughout.

■ **Follow up after the session.** When you see them doing the skill ensure you continue to give encouragement and feedback. Especially for larger, more demanding tasks.

Of course, you don't always have to give feedback. Sometimes just asking "Why do you think that happened?" or "What do you need to change?" gets the answers you want. Asking good questions gets the trainees to talk through the skill. The more they talk – and think - it through, the more they understand.

Training builds relationships and demonstrates your commitment to staff.

2.4

Know how to coach

Responsibility and ownership – if every employee demonstrated these two qualities, how much easier management would be! One way that will really encourage these qualities is coaching.

Don't confuse coaching with training. Training is about putting knowledge into someone. Coaching is drawing knowledge out with questions that inspire the coachee to think through and solve issues from their own experience. One great coaching technique is GROW, pioneered in John Whitmore's book *Coaching for Performance*.

"When I want to, I perform better than when I have to"

John Whitmore, racing driver and performance coach

case study Pierre was an outstanding salesperson. However, he ran into trouble when he was asked to coach other salespeople. He became impatient when waiting for answers to his coaching questions – the coachees simply weren't as fast in their

■ **G = Goal.** What is the goal that you want the coachee to achieve? Is it a short-term or long-term goal? Will you share the goal with the employee?

■ **R = Reality.** What is happening now? How aware is your coachee of the behaviours they are currently employing? What are the underlying reasons for their behaviours?

■ **O = Options.** What are the alternative behaviours available to the coachee? What are the merits – or disadvantages – of each option?

■ **W = Will (or way forward).** What option have you chosen and how will you achieve it? What are the obstacles that you must overcome? What help will you need?

Coaching is all about asking questions in a structured, searching way. For instance, during the 'Reality' stage, I might ask, "So what's happening now?" "Why do you think that's happening?" "What effect is that having on your work?"

These questions make the coachee analyse the situation and come up with their own solutions. After all, we all prefer our own solutions to problems!

Coaching is a powerful way of building accountability in your people.

thought processes as him. Eventually he started to prompt the coachees with answers he was looking for. He even began to ask questions that they could only say yes or no to. Great performers do not always make great coaches.

2.5

Keep on track with feedback

"How am I doing?" This question is so important. People want feedback but they want it to be delivered sensitively and effectively.

Sometime we give feedback that's positive and says: "I love what you've done, keep doing it!" Sometimes we give feedback to make someone even better at what they are doing: "I like this but adjusting this would really help". Of course it's the second type of feedback, developmental feedback, that most managers struggle with.

If you have to give feedback to improve someone's performance then go with these six simple steps.

1 **Clarify why the behaviour is happening.** "Renu, I noticed that you haven't started preparing your presentation."

2 **Confirm what your understanding was.** "I thought we agreed that you'd have a session plan completed yesterday."

3 **First recap the benefits of the agreed behaviours.** "You'll remember we agreed that it would help you decide how much time to dedicate to each area?"

4 **State your concern.** "I'm concerned that you might fall behind and have too much to do before the presentation itself."

5 **Ask the employee to confirm.** "What was your understanding when we last spoke about this point?"

6 **Conclude with a positive statement.** "It's your big opportunity Renu, let's make sure that the senior team realise how great your project went."

You must give feedback as close to the event as you can. I call this 'fresh feedback'. There's a time when feedback is ripe and a time when it's too far past its sell-by date! And sometimes you have to assess how receptive the employee will be. If Renu's presentation was a disaster then you may want to wait until she is more receptive to receiving feedback.

One last point: make your feedback specific. Talk about behaviours that people can change and make sure that you never use feedback as an excuse for a personal attack.

Well delivered feedback removes blind spots in people's performance and increases motivation.

2.6

Let others share the load

You can't do everything. You've got to share your work where you can. Not only does it take the pressure off you, you'll find staff enjoy the new responsibilities you've given them. So show your trust in people - follow these seven 'must-do' delegation tips:

1 **Think carefully about who you're going to delegate to.** Don't overload the highest performer. Make sure everyone has the skills to do what you're asking them to do.

2 **Meet quickly with the people you've chosen.** They'll need more time than you to prepare for the task. What might take you a day to achieve might take someone else a week!

one minute wonder Think about the last time your own boss delegated a task to you. What can you learn from the way you were delegated to? How will it change the way you delegate to others?

3 **Set aside plenty of time to talk through the task.** Others may not be as quick in understanding it as you. Allow plenty of time to make things clear.

4 **Be clear about about the end result.** If you only want a one-page report then say so. Be precise about what you're asking someone to do.

5 **Agree how often an employee is going to report back.** Remember, an inexperienced person will need to report back more often than someone who has done the task before.

6 **Ask the employee to summarize what you've asked them to do.** It's a great test of how well they've understood the task!

7 **Let them get on with it.** Don't 'hover' over them. Constantly checking up on their progress shows that you don't really trust them. Stick to the agreed stages of reporting back.

The most important thing about these tips is that they make you think ahead. The worst managers don't plan their delegation – and because the results are so disappointing, the experience often discourages them from delegating ever again. Whatever time you invest in planning your delegation will soon be repaid. Best of all, you will then have more time to get working on the things that interest you!

Delegation is one of the most powerful tools you have to develop your people.

2.7

Orchestrate a winning performance

Your success or failure depends on the ability of your people to deliver high levels of performance. Think of yourself as a musical conductor. The way that you manage your orchestra makes all the difference. Is the performance you're getting music to your ears?

When you manage people, you need to be clear to them about what an excellent performance actually is – to set objectives in terms of quality or quantity or both. Answer the following questions:

1 **What are you aiming for?** What are the objectives you've agreed with your boss? What are the measures that will tell you whether you've been successful or not?

2 **What must you do to achieve your targets?** What activities must you organize to ensure that the team hits the targets?

one minute wonder How responsible do your staff feel for your team's targets? Can they communicate them to you? Are they clear about what they are, how they are measured and when they need to be achieved? If they can't communicate this, how confident are you that they are working effectively towards them?

3 **How are you going to measure progress against your targets?** What systems can you develop that will track how successful the team is against the targets. Will you need reports? Feedback meetings? Presentations?

4 **How are you going to deal with problems that arise?** What if a key employee is ill? Or other priorities emerge? Think ahead and brainstorm likely problems and solutions with the team.

Managers who get performance management wrong often make two mistakes. The first is that they are not clear enough about what they expect of each individual. The second is they don't help their people when they are struggling to perform at the required level.

Great managers care about what's important to their employees, which often makes their employees care about what's important to the manager. They create a culture of openness and honesty: if employees have bad news about performance then the manager needs to know. They don't want to hear about any problems from their boss first!

Good managers consistently deliver against their targets.

2.8

Accentuate the positive in appraisals

A well run appraisal can give a whole new surge of energy to an employee, fire them up to achieve and motivate them to take on new challenges. Is every appraisal like this? No. But they could be if all managers followed these eight easy appraisal tips.

1 **Preparation is everything.** Prepare evidence of achievement. Prepare evidence where the appraisee underperformed. Talk to colleagues and customers. Keep notes of performance between appraisals and refer to them before the big day.

2 **Ask the appraisee to prepare for the appraisal.** They should come with their own evidence of achievement and disappointments. Give them at least a week to prepare.

3 **Open the appraisal by acknowledging their contribution.** Positive openings set the tone. Say that it's also an opportunity to put together a development plan.

4 **Review last year's objectives.** Go through what was achieved and what wasn't. What were the highlights? What wasn't achieved? What were the things that got in the way?

5 **Look forward to the challenges of the coming appraisal period.** What business goals are there? How will the appraisee contribute? What plans must you make together?

6 **Review any training.** Was it useful? What have they applied? What training will be needed to meet the challenges ahead?

7 **Agree the key objectives and milestones.** Ask the trainee to summarize what's been discussed. What will be the first challenges? What are the first obstacles to be dealt with?

8 **Finish on a high.** Tell them what happens next with the documentation. Say how much you've enjoyed the session. Then give them a sincere thank you for the hard work that they do.

What to avoid? Never refer only to recent events. You must appraise for the whole appraisal period. Always be fair – we sometimes can be easier with those we like more. And remember to get the appraisee talking most of the time. Self-appraisal can be powerfully effective.

Begin appraisals with a positive tone by discussing achievements.

2.9

Absence won't make the heart grow fonder

There are days when people are genuinely too ill to go to work. And days when some people just can't be bothered to go to work. How can you tell the difference? Sometimes you can never know. But I promise you can lower absenteeism by following these steps.

1 **Record all absences.** You must keep records of attendance. After all, you are probably recording everything else, so why not record the attendance you get from each employee?

2 **Calculate the lost time rate.** Take the total absence (in hours or days) and multiply by 100. Then divide this figure by the available hours or days to arrive at the lost time rate.

one minute wonder Take a moment to think about how you behave when an employee returns to work. How impartial are you? How well do you listen to the reasons given for absence? How easy does the employee find it to talk to you?

3 **Analyse the rate of absence.** Is there an area of the business driving high absenteeism? Is there a reason for this? Workload? Working conditions perhaps? Maybe even a bullying manager?

4 **Agree an absence policy.** If your organization doesn't have one, develop it yourself (remember local employment legislation, though). Employees will then be clear about what you require them to do when they are absent.

5 **Conduct a short 'return to work interview'.** What was the reason for their absence? Is the reason given justified? Are there doubts you need to raise?

What about long-term absence? Well, you have to be careful. Phoning an employee every day at home might look like pressurizing them to return and is not accepted in some countries. But there are valuable things you can still do. Keep in regular contact, and ask relevant questions about their medical condition. Keep them up to date with developments at work so that they still feel involved in the team. Lastly, if the absence is very prolonged, explore other areas of employment within the organization where a disability may not be such a problem.

In 2008 a number of organizations (as part of a study) introduced the above procedures. In 2009 many reported a reduction in absenteeism between 10.2% and 43.4%.

Absence might be due to other issues besides illness.

2.10

Make discipline a quiet word

Very few managers like having to do it. But dealing with behaviour or performance that isn't meeting standards is part of our job. So take courage and be positive in how you deal with discipline.

Wherever you live in the world you will have guidelines or rules for dealing with underperformance in employees. It's usually a combination of company rules and national laws.

You might be tempted to think that the easiest solution is to get rid of someone who is underperforming or being difficult, but is that really the best option? People who underperform usually fail to deliver in one of two areas: they lack ability or they lack the right attitude. Make sure you know what you're dealing with before you act. So ask for a 'quiet word with them' and talk in private.

one minute wonder Think through the likely results of not dealing with discipline issues. Will employees like you more? Will employees thank you for not dealing with people problems? If you don't deal with it, will any problem get better or worse?

> **"**A culture of discipline is not a principle of business; it is a principle of greatness**"**

Jim Collins, American business consultant

Use my 1-2-3 of getting people back to their best.

1 **Agree that there is a performance gap.** What is the difference between what you expect and what the employee is giving you? Are they aware that there is a gap?

2 **Agree the reasons why the performance gap exists.** What is it that has created the behaviour? Why?

3 **Agree how you are both going to close the performance gap.** What actions can you both commit to and over what timescale? When will you meet again to assess their progress?

Before you meet, decide exactly what it is that you are going to deal with. Have examples ready when they have failed to meet standards. Think carefully about how you and they will react. If you're new to management then get a friend to role-play with.

Failing to deal with people issues early will always create bigger people issues in the future.

Make things happen

This chapter asks managers to define tasks clearly for the team, set key milestones and skilfully monitor progress against those milestones. By doing this we impose order and control. We also reduce the likelihood of stress not only for ourselves but also for those who report to us. If there's one theme that links so much of this chapter then that theme is preparation.

3.1

Make the decision to be decisive

Management is so often about making tough decisions. Believe me, you have to be systematic and ask yourself searching questions. The following approach will lead you to good decision-making.

■ **What is the decision you must make and what is the goal?** Clearly state the decision that you must make. What will be the effects of the decision? What goal are you trying to achieve?

■ **What are the facts surrounding the decision?** What information do you already have? What could you find out? Sometimes all the facts may never be made available to you.

case study When I was a new manager, my boss gave me one great piece of advice. "Remember that your team loves a good decision. Your team will often forgive a bad decision. But they'll never forgive no decision." She was so right. Going back over my career, the most frustrated I've sometimes

> ## "We know what happens to people who stay in the middle of the road. They get run down"

Aneurin Bevan, Welsh politician

■ **What are the alternative courses of action?** What other choices might you develop – perhaps through creative thinking?
■ **What value does each alternative action have?** What are the positives and negatives of each decision? Can you develop a ranking for each? How might you assess the impact of each alternative?
■ **How do you implement the decision?** Who must you inform of the decision that's been taken?

Brainstorming with other people often produces ideas that just aren't possible when a manager tries to solve a tough issue on his or her own. Consulting others is always another option. Try and find someone who's been through a similar situation. They may just have the information you need!

Decision-making calls for logic, calm and reason, not emotion.

seen people is when they get...nothing. "Let me get back to you on that" can frustrate an employee. If you have to postpone a decision, make sure it's a genuine postponement. Too often, it's a tactic to avoid making a decision and hoping that everyone forgets about the question.

3.2

Project plan, plan, plan

Let me give this to you straight. Projects demand excellent planning skills. There are three critical factors that you will have to plan for: time, cost and quality. Of course, at the centre of all of this are people. You don't want to waste their time. And you certainly don't want them to waste yours.

When I'm running project management workshops most of the time is given over to project definition and planning skills. I know that the time taken on defining and planning projects will have a huge pay-off when the project is implemented.

A project has a start and finish date. Often it's a series of actions that help you achieve a specific objective. The person you've agreed this objective with is the project sponsor. You will have agreed a specific outcome, a deadline and the resources you will need.

"A man who does not think and plan long ahead will find trouble at his door" Confucius, ancient Chinese philosopher

There are four key stages in a project.

1 **Definition.** What is the outcome the project must achieve? You must make sure that this has been exactly defined and agreed. Write a document which says what the project will deliver with what resources.

2 **Planning.** How are you going to achieve the outcome? Draw a plan of the project's key stages. Then break these down into detail. This will help you accurately calculate the time and resources.

3 **Implementation.** How well is the project going? How accurate was your planning? Were your estimates correct? What unforeseen problems must you deal with? Are you managing the expectations of your sponsor?

4 **Closure.** Have you delivered the outcome successfully? How well did the project go? Is work still outstanding? Did your sponsor change the outcome during the project? What have you learned for future projects?

Many believe that a project is 70% people skills. Elsewhere in this book you'll get plenty of help with these. A great project manager is also assertive, charming, demanding, approachable, driving, understanding, detail-driven, trusting, challenging... It's a long list! That's why great project managers are so rare.

Successful project managers spend as much time as possible defining and then planning their projects.

3.3

Object to unclear objectives

Get this area wrong and managing people can be very difficult. The ability to set clear objectives is one of the most important skills to master. It makes people concentrate on achieving the right things. Achieving objectives builds self-confidence. They bring focus to all that you and your people do.

Great objectives meet the SMARTER criteria.

■ **S = Specific.** The objective must apply to a particular area of work. If it's too vague then the employee may feel it's impossible to achieve.

■ **M = Measureable.** It's important for employees to have a clear idea of what success will be. Most measures are usually related to quality, quantity or accuracy.

■ **A = Agreed.** It's critical that the employee 'signs up' to the objective. They need to commit to achieving the goal. They own the objective.

■ **R = Realistic.** Don't try to impose an objective that sets up an employee to fail. Yes, it's got to stretch them, but it mustn't be impossible to achieve.

■ **T = Time-bound.** When is the objective going to be completed by? Giving the objective a clear time frame focuses the employee on planning to achieve it.

■ **E = Extending.** Employees need to be stretched. So the objective has to inspire them to raise their performance towards a challenging goal.

■ **R = Recorded.** It's important to write down what objectives are being agreed. The manager and employee will always have the original objectives to refer back to.

Write objectives using 'action' verbs. Examples of action verbs are: 'to present', 'to sell', 'to write', etc. All of these verbs are easy to attach a measure to. Avoid vague verbs such as 'understand'.

So let's write an objective. We might agree: 'By the end of January you will have entered new customers' contact details onto the sales database with no more than three instances of incorrect data entry.' This objective is about a specific task (data entry), has a target date for completion (end of January) and a quality measure (three errors).

Well written objectives focus employees and increase their sense of self-esteem when they achieve them.

3.4

Identify meaningful milestones

Many employees can be unrealistic about how long work takes. Some give wildly optimistic deadlines. Helping them to arrive at sensible work schedules is an important management task. Working out timelines and milestones can be very helpful.

■ **Timelines.** A timeline is a sequence of events usually in order of time. It's often shown as a continuous line (usually drawn left to right) with significant points along it.

case study As a young, very busy manager I was asked by the senior team to develop a database. Something to bring together customer information kept on separate systems. I asked Paul to do the task as he was good with technology. We agreed a completion date and, being so busy, I just let him

■ **Milestones.** A milestone is a target on the timeline which must be achieved. Each milestone usually concludes a significant piece of work. They're great because they indicate how much progress is being made. Asking an employee to give you an estimate for a large task with a timeline and milestones gets them to think about detail.

I might say to someone: "Anna, I'd like you to organize this year's conference. I want an estimate of how long the whole task will take. I also need a diagram of how you will carry the task out and each major phase. Please show how long you think each phase will take and target dates for their completion."

As Anna carries out the task, I'll know how well it is going by monitoring her progress against each milestone. Milestones act as an early warning system. If they start to be missed, we can act quickly to get the task back on schedule.

Milestones are important indicators of a task's progress.

get on with it. "How's the system coming along?" I'd regularly ask. "Fine", he'd reassure me. After a few weeks I discovered that he was struggling with the task and was way behind schedule. Every job from that day forward had a timeline and milestones!

3.5

Make your monitoring effective

Have you seen the popular definition of the difference between being efficient and effective? Being efficient is doing things right. Being effective is doing the right things. A manager's job is to make sure employees keep on doing the right things.

When we monitor someone what we should be doing is ensuring that they are making progress towards reaching their goals. We need to know how employees are coping and if there are any issues or problems we need to be aware of.

Highly controlling managers always make sure employees know who's 'in authority'. They constantly check and recheck progress. Eventually people feel that there is no trust and often become demotivated. A good manager knows how important it is to be trusting and approachable. They believe themselves to be 'an authority' to their people. Their style is 'I'm here if you need me.'

A casual "Sven, how's the project coming along?" is friendly and interested. Imagine if the question had been, "Sven, I'm worried you haven't even finished the scoping yet." It could be seen as doubting whether Sven's got things under control.

"You may be deceived if you trust too much, but you will live in torment if you do not trust enough" **Frank Crane, American columnist**

Here are some helpful tips when monitoring work:

1 Have one-to-ones each month and ask for progress against the agreed targets and milestones.

2 Raise any concerns you have in a positive way. For example "Sven, are you happy you've got enough time for the testing phase?"

3 Ensure employees know that you're available should they need your input.

4 Create an atmosphere of openness and honesty so that people feel comfortable sharing their anxieties.

5 Be observant and ready to intervene should an employee look stressed or anxious.

You have to strike a balance when you monitor employees' work. As a guide, you need to monitor someone closely if they are new or struggling to perform a task. Higher performers can be monitored less. If you have agreed clear goals and a sensible timeline with good milestones, then you should be able to let them get on with it.

Monitoring high performers too closely may destroy trust.

3.6

Assign fair shares

A fair manager treats people equally and assigns work equally. But this can be a delicate subject because not every employee is equally talented. How can you make sure you don't break the back of your high flier but still get a full contribution from the less talented?

Am I going to talk about planning again? Yes I am! If you don't think carefully about how you give out work then you'll soon find you have one person crushed by their workload, while sitting beside them is someone with nothing to do. So here's how to do it.

1 **Assess your staff's strengths and weaknesses.** What particular talents does each individual have? What things don't they do well? What type of work really gets them buzzing?

one minute wonder How fair is the workload spread across your team? Is everyone equally busy? Have you made sure that you haven't given all of the interesting work to one individual? Is everyone equally challenged by the work they have?

"Be fair with others, but then keep after them until they're fair with you" Alan Alda, American actor

2 **Plan what work is needed to be done and by when.** What are the timelines and milestones for each task? What skill sets will each task demand? Could some tasks be broken down and shared?

3 **Assign the work.** Have you agreed a start and finish date? Have you asked for a timeline and milestones from the individual? Have you agreed how the task will look if it's been successfully completed?

4 **Monitor the progress of each task.** Was the task started on time? Have the early milestones been achieved? Is the member of staff comfortable with the task?

People love doing the work they do best. But sometimes it isn't always possible to assign work that is going to 'wow' them. But we can still make the work important by telling the individual why we have chosen them to do it. It can still be motivating to say, "Ben, I know you always say you hate detail. But you have a great eye for spotting mistakes. I need someone I can completely trust to make sure we don't let this spreadsheet go out with errors."

You must plan carefully before assigning work to your team.

3.7

Write reports that people want to read

Nothing's easier to postpone than writing a report. You do the interesting research. Meet interesting people. But now you have to put it all in writing. It's a tough call for a manager. But by planning the whole process the job won't seem so difficult after all.

Every organization has its own layout for reports. Just look around and find one written by someone else. If the report was a hit, then steal the structure. It's often a variation of the following.

- Title page
- Contents list
- Executive summary
- Introduction

case study Anil was asked to write a report and to have it on his manager's desk by 9am on Monday morning. He worked all over the weekend and produced a closely argued document running to

- Discussion
- Summary and conclusions
- Recommendations
- Appendix

But the real skill is how you organize yourself to write the report.

Think about your audience. Who is the report intended for? What level of formality? Who else may read it?

How detailed is the report expected to be? Are you expected to produce a single sheet with a recommendation on it or a thick document that can be studied?

Decide the purpose of the report. Is it to help other people make a decision? Are people expecting the recommended decision in the report itself?

Who will you need to help you in your research? Who must you consult? Does your research reflect a balance of different opinions?

Map out the information on paper. This will help you in the overall layout of the report and make sure that your reasoning is logical.

Divide the work up into sections giving each a start date and finish date. Start the report by writing your introduction. Then turn to writing the 'summary and conclusions' section. It will really help with writing the rest of the report afterwards.

An interesting report is one that is written with the reader in mind.

nearly 80 pages. He gave it to the manager who went straight to the costs page and said "Oh, we can't afford that", then placed it straight into his out tray. All the manager wanted was a cost estimate!

Communicate in all directions

If ever there's an exercise on a training course that asks for the essential management skills, I can guarantee that the word 'communication' will be very high on the list. Many people think communication is just another word for speaking, but listening and body language are equally important. This chapter touches upon many different aspects, including communicating with your boss, peers, staff and people from other cultures.

4.1

Manage up like you manage down

So often when we talk about management we automatically think of managing those who report to us. But what about managing upwards? After all, the boss can make your life so much sweeter. There are some real skills needed here – and you have to carefully think through your approach.

I love the website www.badbossology.com. Especially their survey which found that "48% said they would fire their boss if they could. 29% would have their boss assessed by a workplace psychologist. 23% would send their boss for management training!"

So is your boss a saint or a sinner? Either way you have to build a relationship that secures a more enjoyable working life. So let me share some helpful insights with you.

■ **Get to know the boss's goals and challenges.** Your boss has goals just like you. Find out and remember them. It's easier to win more resources if they can deliver targets for your boss.

■ **Get to know the boss personally.** How does he or she like to work? What are his or her interests, likes or dislikes?

> **"**I love strawberries, but fish love worms. So when I go fishing I bait my hook with worms**"**

Dale Carnegie

■ **Set goals together.** You need to make sure that you're working on the right things. Don't just update your boss with your achievements. Let him or her know where you'll next be prioritizing your attention.

■ **Avoid surprises.** No one wants to hear bad news. If you've got a suspicion that something's not going as planned then let the boss know – fast!

■ **Talk in their language.** Every boss has a way of processing information. Some like headlines. Others like bottom lines. Find out and learn their language.

■ **Deliver on your commitments.** It's a rare boss who complains about a high achiever in their team. Deliver against your objectives and your boss's respect for you will rocket.

■ **Go to your boss with solutions – not just problems.** Isn't that what you want from your staff? Show the boss that you've thought things through, even if you both come up with a different answer.

Learn the language of your boss and speak that language every time.

4.2

Turn on your feedback channel

We all have blind spots. Whenever I meet someone from college I think: "Wow, you're looking old." I'm stupid enough to think I still look like I did when I was at college! So getting good feedback does you a big favour. You wake up to reality. After all, you may be about to do something disastrous…

Getting high quality feedback starts with your staff. Just because they may not be telling you anything doesn't mean you're doing a wonderful job. So let them know you welcome feedback. But don't give them a question that is easy to say 'no' to. Asking 'Can I improve the

case study The second time Rory was turned down for promotion he was angry. He looked again at the job description and was sure that he had the experience and skills. Rory thought the interview went well. There had to be something else. At a company conference he had a few drinks with his boss, Joy. With a few drinks, tongues loosened and Rory

way I do my job?' may prove too big a question for many. Make it easier for them, with questions such as these:

■ "What could I do more of to help you?"
■ "What one thing could I do that would really help you in your work?"
■ "What could I work on that would bring the most benefit to our team?"
■ "What do you most want from me?"

Once you've received the feedback always thank them. A gracious response means that you'll encourage even more honesty the next time you ask. Whatever you do, do not become defensive. There's no better way of closing down that feedback channel once and for all.

And what about feedback that's just not true? It happens. Well, it's exactly the same response. Whatever you might think, this is their perception. And perception is their truth. Now you know what you have to change.

Always reply to good or bad feedback with: "Thanks for the feedback".

pressed her why he was passed over for the second time. "Too flippant" was the grudging response. "You think everything's a joke. People just won't take you seriously and it's a serious job." There was Rory's blind spot. What he thought was a light approach to life was viewed as flippancy. From that moment this blind spot became his main focus.

4.3

Get to know yourself

"No man is an island" said John Donne. And no manager is an island. You have to build relationships with people. Not only their direct reports but those drawn from other areas of the organization. There are some pretty basic rules to making sure you have a healthy, thriving network of people around you.

■ **Be genuinely interested in other people.** Dale Carnegie said "The royal road to a man's heart is to talk to him about the things he treasures most." And he's right.

■ **Think before you speak.** If someone annoys you, count to 5 and then ask them a question. Biting back at someone may feel good at first, but the damage lasts well after the event.

■ **Get personal.** I have a family and interests away from the workplace. Get me speaking about them and I'm warming to you straight away. Learn about people's passions outside of work.

■ **Be sensitive to others.** Humour is a tricky thing. You might get a laugh from the group, but the person you've just aimed your humour at could be deeply offended.

■ **Never gossip.** People never tell secrets to a gossiping manager. Your personal credibility is in danger if you talk behind others' backs. If someone tries to gossip to you – move quickly on to another subject.

■ **Build a positive reputation.** Someone once said "The world is full of radiators and drains. Radiators radiate warmth and positivity. Drains just drain it all away." What are you?

■ **Keep your promises.** If you're not sure you can meet a request, say so. Under-promise and over-deliver. Too many people do it the other way around.

■ **Show respect.** We all meet people we don't like. But never show disrespect towards them. Be fair. You suffer their personality for an hour. They suffer their personality 24 hours a day.

We're right back to your values here. If you behave in a respectful, values-driven way then I would put money on your credibility and respect rising rapidly. And I'm not even a betting man.

Showing a genuine interest in people will build you a great network of contacts.

4.4

Questions first – then listen up

Great questioning lies at the heart of so much of what managers do. Think about it: appraisals, interviews, disciplinary reviews, one-to-ones, meetings, decision making. Then after the questioning you have to be able to listen carefully.

Differentiate between open and closed questions:

■ **Open questions.** These give you information and get people talking. They start with who, what, why, when, where and how. If someone is able to reply with a straight 'yes' or 'no' then it's probably closed.
■ **Closed questions.** These include words such as can, would, did, have, will, are, etc. It's a bigger list. As managers we need information to help us make better decisions. Therefore we should be asking open questions most of the time.

A key skill is asking questions but maintaining neutrality. We need to show that we are always open-minded. If I'm having a tough conversation then I need to convey that I haven't already come to a decision. For example: "Riki, why did you upset that customer?" Here,

"Listen or thy tongue will keep thee deaf" Indian proverb

I'm implying that I've already made up my mind it's her fault. Better would be: "Riki, what happened between you and the customer?" This gives Riki the chance to explain her side of the events.

And what is it that great listeners do?

■ **They look like they're listening.** Most people know when you've switched off. And it's insulting.

■ **Their responses show they're paying attention.** What they say is a natural progression from what's been said. It develops and expands the conversation.

■ **They remain neutral.** Don't rush ahead with what you think the speaker might be saying. You'll stop listening the moment you pass judgement.

■ **Their physical response is appropriate to the message.** If the person is telling a funny anecdote they smile. If it's bad news they look serious. Bad listeners often mix up the two!

■ **They don't interrupt.** They make sure that the person finishes. Just jumping in with their opinion too early isn't going to get the conversation anywhere.

The ability to remain neutral when questioning and listening is crucial.

4.5

Always be tactful

Managers often have to choose their words carefully to avoid upsetting people. The ability to control a message can often defuse a difficult conversation. If you don't learn this skill, then you can make a situation worse. First, you have to choose whether to speak at all. Then, you need to clarify the situation and take great care in responding.

What is tact? It's choosing the right thing to say or do without offending. 'Choosing' is the important word here. Tactless people don't exercise that choice. They instantly say what's on their mind – and wish they hadn't. Managers have to filter what they say.

When you're communicating with people, remember that how you say something can build – or break – self-esteem. "Monika, that introduction you did was far too long." How much better if she'd been told: "Monika, there's so much great material in your presentation, I'd shorten your introduction to get to it."

"Tact is the art of saying nothing when there is nothing to say"

Anonymous

When you find yourself in a difficult conversation, follow this TACT approach.

■ **T = Think – don't speak!** Any first rush of emotion soon subsides. Get your brain under control and show interest. Do this and you're 75% of the way there.

■ **A = Ask questions.** There are two reasons for this. First, questioning allows you crucial time to think. Second, you're showing respect by encouraging the person to give their view.

■ **C = Clarify your understanding.** Use clarification questions to check that you fully understand the other person's point of view. "So what you're upset about is…"

■ **T = Talk with care.** Give yourself time and make sure that what you say is neutral. Later on you may give your opinion because you've thought it through. But do you need to do so now?

Finally, let's get one thing clear. Being tactful is not about avoiding confrontation. I still want you to be direct and honest. It's just that I want to make sure people want to listen to you. And that involves not 'turning them off' what it is you're trying to say.

Tact is about exercising choice and control over what you say and do.

4.6

It's great to collaborate

How wide is your network across your organization? Could it be better? If you'd like to increase your influence, then building collaboration with other managers is the answer. This takes a certain sort of thinking called 'Abundance Mentality'. It's a trait that will mark you out as a person with a special attitude.

The phrase 'Abundance Mentality' was first used in Stephen Covey's book *The Seven Habits of Highly Effective People*. It describes an attitude that there are plenty of resources and success to go round. It's the opposite of the 'Scarcity Mindset'. You know the type. Those who think that there isn't much to share, so they spend their time hiding the little they believe they have.

■ **Collaborative managers.** These managers are essentially positive. They take people at their word and look to strengthen their links – and influence - across the organization. They have good feelings of self-esteem. They feel secure in what they do and don't fret about who gets the credit for what.

"Only when we join with others do our gifts become visible, even to ourselves"

Margaret Wheatley and Myron Kellner-Rogers, business consultants

■ **Bonds of trust.** Because collaborative managers are so positive they attract like-minded people to them and build strong bonds of trust. They make gestures to other managers. Release resources that they know another manager really needs. Do favours but ask for nothing in return. They think about the interests of both the customer and the organization for which they work.

■ **The enemy of collaboration.** Cynicism and competitiveness are the enemies of collaboration. Competitive managers focus on their own gains. They build a 'bunker mentality' in their team and are cynical about the good intentions of others. Because they believe 'knowledge is power' they keep information to themselves, even when it could potentially damage key initiatives or relationships.

So the choice is yours. But be aware: not every attempt to build collaboration will be met positively. Competitive managers will be very cynical about you. But the good people you link up with will more than make up for any disappointments along the way.

Collaboration with other managers will extend your reach and influence.

4.7

Be a culture vulture

The world seems to be getting smaller; people talk of the 'Global Village'. International companies expect managers to be 'Glocal'. Many have the wonderful opportunity to mix with people from different cultures. But we have to be aware that an increased awareness of those cultures calls for real sensitivity.

Cultures are so much more than food, customs or language. Different cultures have codes that are not immediately apparent. Understanding these codes and responding intelligently to them is a challenge for even the most travel-weary manager. Learning to work with people from other cultures can be vital for a manager.

Here are some tips that will help you make sense of the different cultures and codes you might encounter.

■ **Find out as much as you can in advance.** The Internet is a wonderful place to find out about other cultures. Talk to anyone you know who has already worked with people from the other culture.

■ **Live with ambiguity.** Not all cultures are easy to understand. You have to take your time and this can be tiring. But such patience is often well rewarded.

> **"**Diversity is not about how we differ. Diversity is about embracing one another's uniqueness**"**

Ola Joseph, Nigerian-born inspirational writer

■ **Watch and learn.** Note carefully how people in the other culture interact with each other. How they dress. How they talk together. You're bound to observe clues that help refine your interactions.

■ **Investigate with questions.** Many people enjoy talking about their culture with others. So ask questions. Take an interest. They'll certainly notice it – and appreciate your efforts and interest.

■ **Slow down.** It's frustrating when we speak at our normal pace. Especially to those who do not share our language. Ask them to interrupt you if you talk too fast.

■ **Be careful with humour.** Humour doesn't travel well so, if in doubt, don't use it.

■ **Don't generalize.** You'll find many different personalities in your own culture. Expect the same in others. If someone is quiet it may not necessarily be a cultural thing. They're probably just a quiet person!

■ **Check your assumptions.** Ask people you work with about the conclusions you might be reaching about a certain culture. It's a great 'sense check'.

Find out all you can in advance about working with people in other cultures.

4.8

Learn the language of body talk

It's important for managers to read body language, especially in emotional or testing situations. It's also vital to consider how gestures are interpreted in different countries and cultures.

Unfortunately there are a lot of myths about body language. For example you might see a person folding their arms. "Interesting" – you might think – "that person is obviously being defensive." Not necessarily so, if it's in isolation. If you want to understand body language you must first realise that you look for clusters. A cluster is a combination of different postures and gestures.

■ **A typical cluster.** How do you show your staff you are being attentive? Well, you tend to stay still and even lean forward. Often, your head tilts slightly to one side and you look directly at who's talking. If there are distractions, you'll tend to ignore them. If you're concentrating you'll have a furrowed brow.

■ **Don't over-act your own body language.** Don't start trying to change your own body language if you are already a good listener. It's wrong to not listen because we're concentrating on looking like we're listening! But do look for it in people you're talking to.

■ **Body language in other cultures.** Gestures often mean different things in different countries. You'll find a friendly thumbs up is a positive gesture in the USA. Do it in Bangladesh, though, and the person you're talking to will be deeply insulted. Eye contact is important in many European countries, whereas prolonged eye contact in some Asian cultures creates a very negative effect.

As the world gets smaller, things are slowly changing. In Japan the common greeting is bowing. But you'll find that some Japanese business people are quite comfortable with a handshake. Especially those who work internationally.

Make sure that you use a body language that respects another person's culture. Find out how to align your posture, eye contact and the distance you stand or sit to that person without causing offence.

Look for clusters, not single gestures, in someone's body language.

4.9

Write emails with care

People seem to forget that an email says so much about them. It can convey personality and management style, and even level of respect for the recipient. So emails should be written with care. It's a permanent reminder of the person who wrote it. Let me share with you the email etiquette I subscribe to.

■ **Match the style of the sender.** If someone's direct - I send them direct emails. If someone's friendly, then notice how much warmer my emails are.

■ **Read the email properly before you reply.** You want to save yourself from getting involved in long exchanges. So make sure your reply covers all of the relevant points raised.

■ **Keep sentences short.** Studies show that only 4% of readers understand a sentence of 27 words. 75% of readers understand a sentence of 18 words. 95% of readers understand a sentence of 8 words.

■ **Structure and layout.** It's easier to read from a sheet of paper than it is to read from a computer screen. So lay out your email clearly.

■ **Don't include everyone in your replies.** Do you enjoy getting emails that aren't relevant to you? Then make sure you don't do it to others!

■ **If it's complicated then pick up the phone.** Better still, go and see the other person. It's quicker and a more effective use of your time.

■ **Keep the subject line relevant.** Especially when you're involved in long email exchanges. So change it to reflect any new content.

■ **Never write an email in anger.** We know to avoid speaking when angry. It's the same with emails. If you can, leave it overnight and then reply – calmly.

■ **Fill in the 'To' box last.** As long as there is no email address in the 'To' box, then an accidental slip isn't going to be disaster for you.

Research has shown that men are three times more likely to offend in an email than a woman. Apparently, men just don't see the potential insult! Women are much more alert to the way a sentence might be interpreted.

The tone and content of your emails convey a strong image about your level of professionalism.

Recruit the very best

There is a saying: "First-rate people recruit first rate people. And second-rate people recruit third rate people." You want the best candidate available to join your team. To achieve this you have to convince them – by the professional way you interview – that this is the place to be. Unfortunately, not all managers think about this, and their underperforming team is a testament to their inability to recruit effectively.

5.1

Know exactly what you're looking for

The worst way to look for a new employee is to tell yourself: "I'll know what I want when I see it." What you're really saying is "I'm going to choose the person who's most like me." You have to sit down and establish a profile of the person you need. Being objective is the sure way to find the right candidate.

Why is this so important? Well, it's been calculated that the cost of replacing your 'recruitment error' works out to twice their annual salary. So let's concentrate on getting this essential area right.

Draw up a job specification that sets out the qualities and skills the person is going to need for the role. If your organization doesn't already have such a document, then make a list of the following.

■ **What are the key duties of the job?** Make a list of all the duties they will be expected to perform and make sure that you've included things such as who they have to work with.

■ **What are the essential skills needed?** Every job has its 'deal breakers'. These are the 5 – 6 skills a candidate must have in order to be successful.

> **"Recruiting gets a whole lot easier when you have a reputation for being a great place to work"** Joanna Meiseles, founder of Snip-its hair salons

■ **What qualifications must they have?** Do you require a degree or other professional or academic qualification in a certain discipline? Are there other qualifications that you know the person might have if they were thinking of applying?

■ **What level of experience are you looking for?** How much experience would you expect them to have? Do you need someone who is going to make a contribution immediately to your team?

■ **What are the specicific demands of the role?** Are there any specific personal /physical demands? You seldom get fire fighters with a fear of heights. Although I have known some customer service people with no idea of how to speak to customers...

The wonderful thing about this document is that it will make you objective about what you're looking for. As applications start to arrive, you calmly assess each one against this job specification.

If you already have a document of this kind, then let me warn you. They are often out of date. So find someone who already does the job, and check that the specification reflects the current duties.

A well prepared job specification keeps you objective and focused on finding the best candidate for the role.

5.2

Get ready to impress at interview

Great. The job specification is done. Now for the interview itself. Wait! Aren't you forgetting something? Your candidates are going to put a lot into preparing for their interviews with you. Doesn't that mean you also have some serious preparation to do? After all, you have to impress them as well.

You've drawn up a list of skills. You've highlighted the deal breakers they must have for the role. How do you know they have these skills? Just take their word for it? You need to prepare questions that check if they have what you're looking for.

case study A previous manager once taught me the value of preparation when we sat down to prepare questions for a sales position. "Have a go – see what questions you come up with." So I drew up what I thought was a pretty fine list. Deal breakers such as 'persistent', 'excellent communicator', 'persuasive', 'great product knowledge'. I passed the questions

These questions are the opportunity for the candidate to tell you all about their experience. You'll want evidence that they've already done the things you're going to ask them to do. So how you phrase your question is crucial. Here are a couple of examples of what I mean.

■ **Working with difficult people.** If you ask: "Have you experience of working with difficult people?", the candidate can simply reply: "Yes, lots." It tells you nothing and it's also easy for them to lie. Instead make the candidate go back to their experience and give examples of when they've done it. "Tell me about the most difficult person you've dealt with." Now they have to give a full answer.

■ **Working as part of team.** Is a key element in the job description teamwork? Right, try this: "What's the most successful team you've been part of and why?" Follow up with "What was your personal contribution to its success?" Got it?

Your task is to write down 9 or 10 questions of this kind based on the job specification. The answers will give you a picture of the true extent of the candidate's experience and abilities.

Questions that focus on the candidate's past performance give you much greater insight into their ability.

over to him for approval. "So these would be the areas you'd concentrate on?" he asked. "But what about customers?" I realized that my great list had omitted the crucial skill of any salesperson. Their ability to build relationships with customers. That's why you take time to prepare. You might just overlook something vital.

5.3

Save time with a telephone interview

Some candidates look good on paper. But when you interview them you realize their CV was… inventive. You know they're wasting your time and you're wasting theirs. How do you avoid this scenario? Easy – think about telephone interviewing.

CVs don't always give you the information you'd like. It might say that they've experience with a certain type of software. But that could mean anything. First, set up a telephone interview to find out. Then, if they really do have the experience you're looking for, get them in for a normal interview. But let's be careful. Just because it can be time-saving you still need to prepare. Here are some 'must-dos' to make sure you're fully prepared for the telephone interview.

1 **Review the applicant's CV.** What particular areas would you like to explore in more detail? Is it their technical ability? Is it a key area of their personality you need to make sure of?

2 **Review the job specification.** Remind yourself of the core skills, the 'deal breakers' required for the role.

> **"The telephone is a good way to talk to people without having to offer them a drink"**

Fran Lebowitz, American author and columnist

3 **Prepare a structure for the interview.** Write down your questions and decide in which order you will ask them.

4 **Prepare a scoring mechanism.** You need to decide how you are going to assess whether the candidate is suitable or not.

5 **Understand how you are going to record information.** Will you take notes or will you have someone also dialled in to do this for you?

6 **Build in time for any questions you might be asked.** The candidate may well have areas they'd like to explore.

7 **Decide how you intend to close the call.** Will you be offering feedback to the candidate? What is the next stage?

Make sure you call the candidate exactly on time. It should never be 5 minutes too early and any delay should not be more than 2–3 minutes. Also, make sure you put the applicant at ease so that you get the most out of the telephone interview.

Preparation for a telephone interview must be as thorough if it were a face-to-face interview.

5.4

Make great candidates want to join you

If you've already got great questions to ask then this part should be easy. But there are still some pitfalls to avoid. Situations can arise when you suddenly realize that the person you're interviewing is actually in control – not you. So let's just go through some skills that serve to make a great interview.

1 **Always collect the candidate yourself.** You start to build rapport straight away and settle the candidate.

2 **Introduce the other interviewers and say what's going to happen.** Let the candidate know how long the interview will be.

3 **Introduce the skill area before you ask your question.** This just orientates the candidate and lets them know what you're asking about.

4 **When a candidate answers your question, probe for more detail.** Find out why they did what they did. What were the motivations for their actions? How competent do they seem?

5 **'Hide your hand'.** Do poker players show you what cards they've got? Don't smile too enthusiastically when they reply. You'll be giving clues for what you're really looking for from them.

6 **Let candidates have time to respond.** It can be tough thinking of answers. You're not testing their ability to show super-sharp responses. You just want to ensure they have the experience for the job.

7 **Take notes.** If you've got a full day of interviewing you'll need them! Candidates can merge into one another. Good notes make sure you remember key areas of information about candidates.

8 **Don't say things that imply the candidate has got the job.** Always refer to 'the successful candidate'. Never say things like "When you've started you'll be expected to…" That sounds like a job offer!

9 **Don't play 'games' with the candidate.** Being nice one minute and nasty the next can turn an excellent candidate off. Be normal with the candidate. Relaxed candidates give fuller answers.

At the end of the interview, advise the candidate what happens next. This is a basic courtesy. They need to know when you intend to contact them with your next move.

You need to make the interview as professional as possible – you're being interviewed as well.

5.5

Avoid that fatal attraction

The interviews are over. Now you have to choose the best applicant for the role. There are times when the successful candidate is obvious. Or are they? When we interview, we have to be careful that we don't lose the objectivity that prevents us from making the most professional decision.

In a 2008 UK survey 2,266 employers were asked if they had ever given a job to someone because they were the most attractive candidate. A staggering 88% of respondents said yes!

case study Years ago, a friend of mine applied for a role as a Personnel Officer ('Personnel' was the original name for HR). Jacqui was clever, outgoing and great with detail. Perfect for the role. Imagine her disappointment when it went to someone else. In time the successful candidate started. She was like something from the movies. Young and very, very

Let's be clear. In our organizations we have a responsibility to recruit people who will successfully achieve the objectives we are going to set them. Managers who consistently recruit under-performers tend to make life very hard for themselves.

So how do we make sure we assess people fairly and (that word again) objectively? I suggest you rate the experience they communicated in the interview against each skill you decided upon beforehand. It could be something like:

3 – Demonstrated experience of this skill in excess of that required for the role.

2 – Demonstrated experience of this skill that met the requirements of the role.

1 – Demonstrated some experience that would be required of this skill – would probably need training.

0 – Demonstrated little or no experience of this skill.

Now all you have to do is discuss the notes you took from each interview and agree a rating for each candidate. If you have a successful candidate in mind, was this borne out in your ratings for them?

Your choice of candidate communicates your ability to be objective.

attractive. However, she couldn't even spell 'personnel'. Her emails always referred to herself as the 'Personal Assistant'. She also wasn't good at the job. The Personnel Manager became the joke of the organization and he soon followed her out of the company. Recruit for skill. How a person looks seldom has anything to do with a job.

Build a great team

A high-performance team is all about blend. Sports managers spend sleepless nights trying to get this right. It's exactly the same with a work team. Its members have to complement each other. At first they may fall out and fight, but, with a good manager, they work through this and build a spirit that binds them together and makes the best use of their collective skills. Each member of the team understands their role and the roles of their team-mates.

6.1

Define the team roles

Great teams have a mix of skills. Each person brings a different skill set to the task in hand. When a manager has achieved this mix, they have created a team with the potential to deliver real success.

One of the pioneers of understanding the different characters that can exist in a team was Dr. Meredith Belbin. His research established that there were 9 roles.

■ **Implementer.** The team's practical organizer.
■ **Co-ordinator.** The team's natural leader, although they may not be the 'formal' head.
■ **Shaper.** The team's action person and often its formal head.
■ **Plant.** The team's ideas person and an original thinker.
■ **Resource investigator.** The team's liaison person with outside contacts.

one minute wonder Consider the most successful team you have been part of. How broad was the skill set of the team? Looking at the above list, what 'role' did you play in the team? What roles were played by your colleagues?

"You don't get harmony when everybody sings the same note"

Doug Floyd, American journalist

■ **Monitor/evaluator.** The team's judge and often its most objective, uninvolved member.

■ **Team worker.** The team's harmonizer, often referred to as the cement of the team.

■ **Completer/finisher.** The team's checker who compulsively pursues deadlines and detail.

■ **Specialist.** The team's expert, the provider of knowledge and technical skills.

Of course there are other team role theories as well but Belbin remains the most popular. People can bring two or three roles to a team – not just one. For example, the person who has a strong ability to pursue detail can also be the individual who makes things happen.

The skilful manager assesses the broad skill base of their team and looks to see if there are gaps. These gaps are skills that are not yet present in the current team members. Once the gap has been identified the manager works to see how this can be covered. For example, I might have a team full of 'ideas' people. But have no one with the ability to look objectively at those ideas. I might take on this role. Or I might recruit someone who has this skill in their 'skills kit'.

The stronger the presence of different skills – the stronger the effectiveness of the team.

6.2

Take your team on a journey

All teams undertake a journey. This may happen without any of them leaving their chairs. For some teams the destination is success. For others it may be disappointment and a lot of falling out. The difference is the manager. Their skill can really make sure the team finds – and stays – on the right road.

American psychologist Bruce Tuckman identified five key phases of a team's journey:

1 **Forming.** The excitement (and anxiety) of people coming together as a team. Team members get familiar with each other. But don't expect a lot of work to get done!

2 **Storming.** The 'honeymoon's over' phase. Egos clash as different expectations emerge. Ideas get proposed and plans are set out. Morale can dip dramatically.

3 **Norming.** Members get to understand each other. Productivity is OK but could be better. The team establishes routines.

"Talent wins games, but teamwork and intelligence wins championships**"** **Michael Jordan, basketball ace**

4 **Performing.** That's more like it. We now have a truly professional business unit. The team is focused on a common direction. Meaningful results emerge.

5 **Adjourning.** The team disbands and people move on to other things. A time for satisfaction if targets have been met.

At each stage you have a critical role to play. If your team has just formed, then they'll need direction. Persuasively sell the goals and get each individual on board.

When the team starts to storm, there'll probably be conflict brewing – make sure it doesn't happen. Mediate between people. Get big egos to accommodate each other. Give feedback and reassurance.

Once the team is norming, your role switches again. Ensure decision-making processes and tasks are consistent and accepted by all.

It won't be that long before the team is performing. Now you start to 'back off'. A little coaching and advice perhaps. But the team should be working largely without you.

If it's a project team, then you'll eventually get to the adjourning stage. Provide feedback for each member on their performance. You may have to help them look for new challenges on other projects. You act as a 'bridge' to carry them into the next phase of their working lives.

The manager must subtly change their approach at each stage of the journey.

6.3

Fire up the team spirit

Great team spirit doesn't just happen. It's like a relationship – it takes a lot of hard work. There are some simple things you can do to build and maintain a great feeling between your team members. Here is my cocktail of eight spirit-inspiring tips.

1 **Demonstrate your passion for your work.** A lot of team members take their cue from their manager.

2 **Celebrate milestones.** And achievements, goals and whatever you feel like celebrating. It's great to feel successful.

3 **Introduce them to key partners and customers.** Some team members never see what it is they work towards. Visiting a customer? Then take members of your team with you.

case study Even though he tried to make meetings fun and lively, Stefan was having problems building team spirit. I went to meet the team myself. They were a good bunch of people: funny, clever... and quiet. They had great team spirit when Stefan was

4 **Create a self-managing team.** When people know that, together, they share real responsibility. It will create a strong sense of camaraderie.

5 **Incorporate fun that's been generated by the team.** Great teams always have their own humour. Encourage the humour. It's part of the team's language.

6 **Encourage openness.** Cliques can destroy a team and leave people feeling that others are talking behind their backs. Make sure this doesn't happen.

7 **Get rid of the bureaucracy.** That is, the roadblocks that get in their way. Inefficient working practices really pull teams downwards.

8 **Create opportunities for team bonding.** Team days, nights out, meals in restaurants. All of these promote a sense of togetherness.

Demonstrate your commitment to the team and they'll soon imitate you.

out of the room. As soon as he came in they went flat. Stefan bounced around making motivational statements but they all looked embarrassed. Their idea of team spirit was different from Stefan's and he had failed to notice and encourage it.

6.4

Build a supreme team

Team spirit is the fuel that carries people along. But you have to shape and guide the team to turn it into an outstanding collection of people. World-class teams have certain characteristics that lie at the heart of their activities. These characteristics are valued and demonstrated by everyone – including the manager.

1 **Every member of the team wants to achieve their goals.** There's nothing half-hearted about their commitment.

2 **People feel accountable and responsible.** When a team member struggles, colleagues step in immediately to help.

3 **Everyone contributes.** There are no 'freeloaders' in a strong team. Everyone pulls their weight.

4 **Team members use their initiative.** When they are confident about an emerging situation, they can make decisions.

5 **The team is constantly being challenged to higher levels of performance.** The manager knows that the comfort zone will blunt the skill and appetite of the team members.

6 **Innovation and change is viewed as constant activity.** There's no sitting back once goals have been achieved. The team respond positively to the ever-changing environment they operate in.

7 **There is constant evaluation.** Performance is continually assessed against the goals the team are driving towards. The process also involves 'lessons learned' from significant experiences, which will sharpen the team's skills sets.

You might think a high-performance team will always be brimming with the best people. But this isn't always true. Research suggests a team of 'stars' often underperforms. Team members spend more time fighting to be 'top dog' than on achieving the team's goals.

A manager's contribution to enabling a team to flourish is everything. Their purpose and sense of mission is infectious. They must encourage trust and respect across the team. If they detect any communication that lacks respect or damages trust then they act. No high-performance team has ever thrived without these two vital elements.

High-performance teams are deeply committed to achieving their goals.

6.5

Communicate with a virtual team

Managing a virtual or remote team is the toughest test of their communication skills that a manager can face. It calls for an approach that is more trusting. It also demands that the manager be more detailed and defined in their approach. It asks that they switch from monitoring what people do to concentrating on what people achieve.

Let's distinguish between virtual teams and remote teams. A virtual team is one that has people who all report to other managers – not the person managing the team. A remote team may be similarly scattered, but all its members report to the same manager. To avoid a meltdown in trust in your virtual or remote team, follow these rules:

1 **Communicate like you've never communicated before.** Use the technology out there. Make sure your people share information openly and proactively.

2 **Agree clear goals, roles and responsibilities.** Take every opportunity to build trust within the team.

"Coming together is a beginning. Keeping together is progress. Working together is success" **Henry Ford, American motor manufacturer**

3 **Keep your communications simple.** Don't use idioms and nuances that may not be recognized by the whole team. Always check that everybody understands.

4 **Regularly review the situation.** Look at the effectiveness of all communication that passes between the team.

5 **Keep contact levels high.** Regular emails and instant messaging keep team members close.

6 **Be kind with timing.** Remember that differences in time zones have a big impact on the effectiveness of virtual meetings.

7 **Negotiate if necessary.** Virtual team members may have conflicting projects that affect their contribution to yours. Be understanding and negotiate a reasonable agreement.

Managing a virtual or remote team is much like managing a team that shares the same office. You just have to be a whole lot smarter about it. If things go wrong don't duck out of your responsibility. It's so easy to blame the technology or distance between you and your team members. Great virtual managers find out – and fix – what's wrong.

Work to keep the level of contact high in your virtual or remote team.

6.6

Make time to meet

Bringing the team together not only builds spirit and a sense of togetherness, it also allows people to share and discuss. Some managers point out there's no need for their team to meet. After all, they all work in the same room and should be sharing anyway. But that's missing a crucial point about why team meetings are so important.

There are four main reasons why you need to bring the team together regularly.

1 **It gives the team the opportunity to interact.** People can update each other with how tasks and projects are progressing. This type of communication is so important for coordinating the team's activities.

2 **The team can assess and evaluate information.** Not only does the team share information, they can evaluate new information or developments as well. Group evaluation is often more informed and accurate.

3 **The team can make decisions.** A meeting is often ideal to make decisions about future action. It's also a useful forum for resolving disagreements and misunderstandings.

4 **The manager can motivate and inspire the team.** Goals arrived at by the group are often more inspiring than when imposed by the manager. Meetings allow the manager to facilitate group agreements.

If managers are to avoid team meetings going badly then they should be asking themselves questions such as 'Why are we meeting?' 'What are the objectives of the meeting?' 'Has there been enough developments to justify us meeting?'

What you have to avoid is 'meeting for meeting's sake'. You know the types of managers I'm talking about. "I hold a meeting on a Monday because we always meet on Monday!" And people sit there waiting for the meeting to end so that they can get back to their real job. I've sat in on meetings like these – I'm sure you have too!

But why do so many people dislike meetings? Well, meetings can eat in to a lot of valuable 'doing' time. Therefore, it's vital that your people feel that getting together in a meeting is worthwhile.

Your team meetings must be for a useful purpose – otherwise don't meet.

6.7

Produce an agenda

If people have to go to a meeting then they'll first want to see an agenda. Next, they'll want you to keep to the agenda. Agendas are the best way to structure and pace any team meeting. So prepare well in advance and produce the agenda that lets you keep the meeting on topic – and on track.

There are three crucial things you must do before you sit down together for your meeting.

■ **Decide and communicate the objectives for the meeting.**
Even when you're holding regular team meetings, it's important to be clear about what each meeting is trying to achieve.
■ **Decide who, where and when you are to meet.** You may want to invite someone from outside of the team. The best venue should always be booked ahead as far as possible.
■ **Prepare your agenda.** This vital document will let the team know what will happen at the meeting. Each agenda item should indicate the topic to be discussed and how it will be handled.

"Meetings without an agenda are like a restaurant without a menu" Susan B. Wilson, American business consultant

When you put your agenda together, try and structure it this way:

■ **Opening items.** Easy issues to discuss, routine stuff, any business issue which is urgent but brief.
■ **Middle items.** Longer and more complicated or contentious issues. The team will have far more attention during the middle phase of the meeting.
■ **Final items.** Perhaps a guest speaker. Finish off with easy, interesting matters.

Make sure that your agenda is clear about the start and end time for the meeting. State where the venue is and who will be present. Give each agenda item a time. Also, identify on your agenda who from the team will lead each agenda item discussion. Brief this person about your expectations of how you'd like them to facilitate the discussion.

One item that is increasingly rare on modern agendas is 'Any Other Business'. I've never seen the value of this item. My view is: if it's an important item you want to discuss then put it on the agenda. If it's not important enough then let's talk about it outside the meeting.

One last thought. If it's a long meeting, remember to put in comfort breaks and show these on your agenda.

Your agenda gives structure to the meeting and allows you to control input from those attending.

6.8

Turn yourself into a good chair

The success of a team meeting is often down to the level of control the chairperson imposes. It is the chairperson's job to make sure the meeting starts and finishes on time and functions effectively. Control must be established from the outset. So here are seven chairing tips to keep you in the driving seat.

1 **Make sure you start on time.** In some organizations a 10am start is really a 10.15 start. Make sure that your meetings gain a reputation for starting promptly. Latecomers will soon learn!

2 **Begin with the purpose and main objectives.** Refer people to the agenda and highlight the length of time set aside for each item. Also identify who will lead discussion on different items.

3 **If necessary, ask people to introduce themselves.** A simple 'go round' might be needed from the team if you have a guest speaker or other visitor to your meeting.

4 **Confirm a note-taker/timekeeper.** It's best that these roles, if needed, are delegated to others. It allows the chair to concentrate on keeping the meeting moving.

5 **Inform the group of the end time.** Emphasize this at the outset. This will help later on when you remind talkative contributors of the need for them to be brief.

6 **Review items from the previous meeting.** Briefly cover action items carried over from the last meeting.

7 **Keep the opening brief.** The pace you set at the start conveys a sense of urgency and the need to keep the conversation moving. A too 'laid-back' style isn't recommended.

If you're about to hold your first meeting then why not set the 'ground rules' for all subsequent meetings? You set these by asking attendees to agree to standards of behaviour which everyone can sign up to. Examples of ground rules could be switching off phones and blackberries, not interrupting when someone else is speaking, etc. Your job then is to make sure that the agreed ground rules continue to be respected.

A strong opening immediately establishes the chairperson's credibility.

6.9

Open your meeting to all

There are many frustrations when you're in a meeting. One that really upsets people is when one person dominates everything. It's the chairperson's role to make sure this doesn't happen. It's also their role to make sure that the less dominant people have their say. They may not be as loud, but they do have important contributions to make.

A good chairperson is assertive. They involve everyone by using the following techniques.

case study Grace described her team meetings as 'like herding cats'. But I suspected that she was failing to impose herself assertively on her team meetings. I went as a guest speaker arriving promptly for the meeting at 11.30am. I was first to get to the room... and Grace was last. The meeting was then held up as one person had forgotten the

■ Interrupting domineering contributors. They skilfully interrupt with lines such as: "Sara, you've already shared how you feel about this. I'd like to bring in Andrea for her view. Andrea..."

■ Making sure there is a balance of contributions. Some chairs keep a note of who speaks by ticking their name every time they contribute. They can then quickly see who the quieter members are.

■ Bringing in quieter attendees. They use body language to stop a person who's beginning to dominate (a raised palm perhaps). Then they invite someone who has yet to speak.

■ Controlling the order of people talking. They note people wishing to speak and then place them in a queue: "Hazel you respond first, then Corrina and let's finish with Pippa."

■ Inviting people to begin the discussion. "Alan, this is something which is very close to your heart. Give us some background…"

■ Focusing contributions. People often wander away from an agenda item. The skilful chair is alert to this and intervenes: "Ed, let me just pull you back to…"

■ Summarizing conversations. Once people are fully engaged, the chairperson keeps conversation on track using short summaries of discussions.

Your job as chairperson is to make sure that there is a fair balance of contributions from everyone.

artwork she wanted to share. "Creatives are impossible!" Grace apologized. Sure enough, the meeting was exactly as she described. The agenda was incidental to the meeting. Conversations wandered around and we overran alarmingly. Friendliness and warmth were everywhere. But decisions and progress were nowhere to be seen.

6.10

Turn words into actions

You don't want your team just leaving the meeting having had a good time. You need them to be leaving with a resolve to make things happen. Turning words into action makes sure that your meeting is not some ineffective 'talking shop'. Rather it's a place where decisions are made and people take responsibility for ensuring they are implemented.

A friend of mine used to have a joke about action items in meetings. Question: When are action items actioned? Answer: About 10 minutes before the next meeting!

So how do you make sure this doesn't happen in your meetings? Whenever you have discussed an agenda topic, often an action item will start to emerge. An action item is a documented task, event, activity, or action that needs to be implemented. This action item needs:

■ **An owner.** Someone who is going to take responsibility for getting the thing done.

■ **An outcome.** A clear statement of what that action is intended to achieve.

■ **A date.** When the action will be completed.

"When the outcome of a meeting is to have another meeting, it has been a lousy meeting" Herbert Hoover, US President

It is the third element that often doesn't get pinned down. That's why the action item owner is running around trying to get it done 10 minutes before the next meeting.

'Talking shops' are those meetings where the chairperson lets the group discuss issues at length but no action is ever proposed. But action items are vital because they give meetings a sense of purpose. They are new challenges that take the team closer to delivery of their goals. To adapt Winston Churchill's phrase, action items are about war-war not jaw-jaw.

So make sure that all attendees are clear about what is expected of them and when you will want to see results by.

Most organizations don't have 'Minutes of the Meeting' any more. They see them as time-consuming and too formal. Many prefer the more modern and dynamic 'Action Agendas'. An Action Agenda is a list of action items agreed at the meeting showing who is responsible for what and by when.

As chair of the meeting, it is important to get the action agenda out to the attendees as soon as possible. It can create a real impetus and spur action item owners into… action!

Action items must have a clear outcome, an owner and a delivery date.

Treat the budget with respect

One of a manager's tasks is to help their team see that what they do links in directly with the success of the organization. Success is usually measured in money, and the money you control is your budget. Many think of a budget as a financial 'road map' that gets you to your goals. Once a budget has been prepared the next stage is to negotiate it with the Financial Director. Fail to prepare it properly, and you just might have to go and do it all over again...

7.1

Link in with the strategy

Even though a business strategy is shaped at a senior level everyone has to understand it. The person who is responsible for making sure that front-line employees play their part in the strategy is the manager. They provide the vital link between the senior team and the people who make the strategy happen.

Wherever you work, money is important. Are you in an organization that has to make a profit? Perhaps you're in a 'not-for-profit' organization? Either way, your challenge is trying to find the most cost-effective methods that contribute to the overall strategy.

There are two levels of strategy. The first is the organizational strategy. Your senior team has put together a long-term strategy which sets out a direction. Where the organization's going and how it gets

"Money's a horrid thing to follow, but a charming thing to meet"

Henry James, American novelist

there. They will have put milestones in place and organized finance to help them achieve the overall goal.

There is also a second strategy – the operational strategy. This is how each area of the business organizes itself to deliver its part of the organizational strategy. The operational strategy sets out the people, resources and processes it needs. You play a big part here. By managing resources wisely and making sure you get the best from your people, you will be effectively contributing to the organization's strategy.

Everything you and your team do is either generating revenue or losing it. What happens when you deal well with a member of staff who is demotivated? Well, they'll soon be back working efficiently. If you fail to deal with them well? Then they'll do less work. Both outcomes have a financial implication.

A major factor in employees' motivation is what is often referred to as 'line of sight'. They should be able to see clearly what it is their team does that contributes to the organization's strategy and understand how that strategy affects the way their team operates. The effective manager will always connect the overall strategy of the business to their team's everyday work.

Managers have to be able to link each individual's activities with the delivery of the organizational strategy.

7.2

Understand your budget

Some people are daunted by the idea of planning and sticking to a budget. But you've always looked after a budget before – it's called your personal bank account. A work budget is no different. You need to show the same care as if the money were your own.

A budget is a plan showing what you're going to spend over a period of time – usually a year. It allows you to track how you're spending your money each month and serves as a kind of 'road map' to help you achieve your goals and targets.

For certain departments, the budget is also what money is expected to come into the organization. A sales operating budget would project the amount of revenue the team expected to generate in the coming period.

Every company has a master budget, often looked after by a Financial Director. Your budget forms part of this master budget.

There will be two other budgets as well. The cash budget manages the immediate cash flow of the organization. The capital expenditures budget is money set aside for individual projects.

one minute wonder Who looks after your team's budget? If it isn't you, then ask your manager to talk you through it. What are the headings they have responsibility for? How often do they review it? How close are they to the original forecasts? If you look after the budget, then why not share this information with your team?

The figures in the budget are expressed in monetary terms within a document such as a spreadsheet. Each budget has a series of headings showing areas you will look after.

Typical areas you might control could be:

■ **Staff costs.** Salaries and other staff costs.
■ **Communication.** Cell phones/mobiles, etc.
■ **Client entertainment.** Money to entertain important contacts.
■ **Stationery and office supplies.** Printer cartridges, paper, pens, etc.
■ **Transport and travel.** Costs associated with travelling.
■ **Training.** Induction of staff, ongoing training, etc.

A budget is usually set out by quarter and/or by month. Some managers' budgets won't change. However, many managers will have to 're-forecast' their budget as the year progresses. If unexpected events occur they'll need to negotiate a change in their budget.

A budget tests a manager's ability to accurately anticipate business needs and trends.

7.3

Anticipate the future

In many organizations, a manager's ability to prepare and perform against their budget is an important performance indicator. If you can prepare an excellent budget and then deliver against it, your credibility will be sky-high. To prepare an accurate budget, you must be able to anticipate the future.

Mention the word 'budget' and many roll their eyes in boredom. But it's an important time when you can think carefully about your department's direction. Done properly, it will help you make better decisions. Best of all, going through the process really gives you a grip on the financial side of running your team.

Get a reputation as a person with a real understanding of how the year ahead will 'play out' and people listen seriously to what you have to say. Also, when you go to the Financial Director asking for more budget, they'll listen because you've delivered the numbers in the past.

So here are my seven guidelines for preparing a great budget.

1 **Talk with the people around you.** Your team, customers, suppliers, everyone who will give you information about what they believe the next 12 months will bring. It's free consultancy!

"Don't agonize. Organize"

Florynce Kennedy, American civil rights lawyer and activist

2 **Plan your budget away from your office.** Don't plan budgets where you're likely to get interrupted. Serious thinking demands peace and quiet.

3 **Make your budget realistic.** Don't put in numbers you know aren't going to happen. You'll only be sent away again by your Financial Director with your forecasting reputation in tatters.

4 **Break down the tasks needed to achieve each business goal.** Doing this increases the accuracy of your final figures. It also helps you convince your FD why you need what you've asked for.

5 **Allow for any inflationary rises.** You've noticed that everything gets more expensive in your home life? Well, it's the same in business – so make allowances.

6 **Build flexibility into your budget.** What will happen for certain? What might happen? You may have to accommodate the unexpected.

7 **Be ready to sell the benefits.** Want more money? Fine, but the FD will, wherever possible, want to see what benefits will be generated. Sell the benefits in financial terms.

If you want an increased budget then you're going to need to show the benefits it will generate.

7.4

Negotiate openly

It can be tough when you go to the Financial Director to negotiate your budget. These days organizations are continually on the look-out for where the next cost savings are coming from. So it's going to get a whole lot tougher! Here are seven tips for negotiating positively with your Financial Director.

1 **Don't make unrealistic projections.** If they prove wrong, your FD may withdraw money from your budget.

2 **Don't forget to check the security of your forecasts.** Even if your forecasts are reasonable, the FD will want evidence as to how you'll achieve them.

case study A Financial Director in an IT organization told me about one difficult manager she'd negotiated with. Gary had kept everything from her. When she asked for more detail on hardware he'd requested, he got defensive, saying, "What do you need to know that for?" But finally he understood.

3 **Work positively with the FD.** You're both just doing your jobs. Being prepared to negotiate means that you will need to be flexible. You may get what you want, but have to compromise as to how and when you get it.

4 **Don't be defensive.** If the FD can't meet a request then be reasonable about it. Don't sulk or refuse to work positively.

5 **Don't hide risk.** Your FD wants the full picture. Don't hold information back because it might work against you.

6 **Don't think of it just as a fight for money.** Your FD will have a lot of requests to consider. You'll win more budget by showing a return on investment.

7 **Don't think your organization has unlimited funds.** Your organization has a finite amount of money. Being unrealistic in your requests will lose you credibility.

The role of the Financial Director is to safeguard the finances in the organization. They want realistic projections and evidence that you've obtained maximum value from your budget.

Negotiate assertively with your Financial Director but also be flexible.

"The moment he saw our meeting as a positive one, he realized it didn't have to be hard work! His project was good. But if he wanted the capital expenditure to finance it then he had to give me more detail. As soon as he saw that then we were able to talk constructively about the venture."

Jargon buster

Absence policy
A set of guidelines prepared by the organization that employees must follow if they are not at work through sickness or injury.

Blind spot
A behaviour – usually negative – that someone demonstrates to others but which they're not aware of.

Collaboration
In management, collaboration is defined as working together (often with someone outside the team) to achieve a goal and secure a business benefit.

Comfort zone
At work, an environment in which someone can carry out their tasks without risk of being challenged. A mental or physical boundary someone stays within.

Competence
The ability to do something well. Carrying out a task to the necessary standard.

Deal breaker
An essential skill or ability that the job holder must be able to demonstrate. Failure to convince an interviewer of being able to do this often indicates that the candidate isn't suitable for the role.

Development path
An agreed set of tasks and training activities which raise a person's competence. Often agreed during an appraisal between a manager and a member of staff.

Evidence
Real examples that represent the level of performance demonstrated by someone. It's usually made up of objective data (e.g. revenue figures, tasks completed, etc.), performance during challenging periods or events and behavioural observation.

Freeloader
A person who is willing to enjoy the benefits generated by the hard work of others, but avoids making any contribution themselves.

Glocal
The ability to think globally but act locally. The desire by multi-national organizations for behaviours and practices to be adapted to the local community they operate in.

Goal
Often a vague end point that someone is aiming for. For example my goal may be to raise the influence of my team across the organization. I would then break this goal down into specific and measurable objectives.

Hide your hand
A technique used by interviewers where they do not convey what answers they are looking for. Achieved by a neutral style of questioning, supported by relaxed body language.

High flier

A highly competent person who often exceeds agreed goals and expectations.

Management style

A range of behaviours - from 'controlling' through to 'empowering' – available to a manager. A successful manager would select the correct style from this spectrum appropriate for the individual they are managing.

Motivation

The enthusiasm someone has for carrying out a task or responsibility. Also the reason or need for making sure a task is carried out.

Objective

Something which has been agreed that someone plans to achieve. Usually an end point of achievement for an individual.

Priority

An activity that receives a higher level of attention over other activities because it is either important, urgent or both.

Projection

A calculation about the future often based on experience of what has happened in the past.

Project sponsor

An individual who is ultimately responsible for the project. Often the person the project manager agrees the definition, scope and outcomes of the project with.

Revenue

The income that an individual, department or organization generates.

Role model

An ideal example of excellent behaviour that one person demonstrates to others. Many high performers purposely replicate the behaviour of role models they admire.

Standard

A level of quality against which the performance of an individual will be assessed.

Strategy

A detailed plan for successfully achieving an agreed goal. Often based on: Where am I now? Where do I want to get to? How will I get there?

Target

A level that someone has agreed to aim for. Targets are intermediate stages towards an overall objective.

Time robber

A task, activity or behaviour that is of low value to your goals. For example: attending an irrelevant meeting.

Further reading

As well as recommending the following books I also have a number of articles and in-house management and employee workshops available at www.mhconsult.com

Adair, John *John Adair's 100 Greatest Ideas for Effective Leadership and Management* (Capstone, 2002) ISBN 978-1841121406

Back, Ken and Kate *Assertiveness at Work* (McGraw Hill, 1999) ISBN 978-0077114282

Belker, Loren B. and Topchik, Gary S. *The First Time Manager* (Amacom, 2005) ISBN 978-0814408216

Bennis, Warren G. and Nanus, Bert *Leadership: Strategies for Taking Charge* (Harper Business Essentials, 2003) ISBN 978-0060913366

Blanchard, Ken and Johnson, Spencer *The One Minute Manager* (Harper Collins Business, 2000) ISBN 978-0007107926

Bowden, John *Writing a Report: How to Prepare, Write and Present Effective Reports* (How To Books, 2008) ISBN 978-1845282936

Burka, Jane B. and Lenora, M. Yuen *Procrastination: Why You Do It, What to Do About It* (Da Capo Lifelong, 2009) ISBN 978-0738211701

Connolly, Mickey and Rianoshek, Richard *The Communication Catalyst* (Kaplan, 2002) ISBN 978-0793149049

Covey, Stephen R. *7 Habits of Highly Effective People: Powerful Lessons in Personal Change* (Simon and Schuster, 2004) ISBN 978-0743272452

Fisher, Kimball and Mareen *The Distance Manager: A Hands on Guide to Managing Off-Site Employees and Virtual Teams* (McGraw-Hill Professional, 2000) ISBN 978-0071360654

Fisher, R. and Ury, W. *Getting to Yes* (Penguin Books, 2008) ISBN 978-1844131464

Foster, Mark *Do it Tomorrow and Other Secrets of Time Management* (Hodder and Stoughton, 2006) ISBN 978-0340909126

Goleman, Daniel *Working with Emotional Intelligence* (Bloomsbury, 1999) ISBN 978-0747543848

Honey, Peter *101 Ways to Develop Your People Without Really Trying* (Peter Honey, 2003) ISBN 978-1902899220

Lencioni, Patrick *The Five Dysfunctions of a Team* (Jossey-Bass, 2002) ISBN 978-0787960759

McGregor, Douglas *Leadership and Motivation* (MIT Press, 1966) ISBN 978-0262130233

Maitland, Iain *Budgeting for Non-Financial Managers: Turn Your Budgeting Strategy into a Valuable Management Tool* (Financial Times/Prentice Hall, 1999) ISBN 978-0273644941

Nelson, Robert B. *Empowering Employees through Delegation* (Longman Higher Education, 1994) ISBN 978-0786301997

Pincus, Marilyn *Managing Difficult People: A Survival Guide for Handling Any Employee* (Adams Media, 2005) ISBN 978-1593371869

Portny, Stanley E. *Project Management for Dummies* (John Wiley, 2007) ISBN 978-0470049235

Senge, Peter M. *The Fifth Discipline: The Art and Practice of the Learning Organization* (Random House Business Books, 2006) ISBN 978-0712656870

Tate, Rick and White, Julie *People Leave Managers...Not Organizations* (iUniverse Books, 2005) ISBN 978-0595779765

Tavris, Carol and Aronson, Elliot *Mistakes Were Made (but Not by Me)* (Pinter and Martin, 2008) ISBN 978-1905177219

Whitmore, John *Coaching for Performance* (Nicholas Brealey Publishing, 2002) ISBN 978-1857885354

Yeung, Rob *Successful Interviewing and Recruitment* (Kogan Page, 2008) ISBN 978-0749451646

www.BusinessSecrets.net